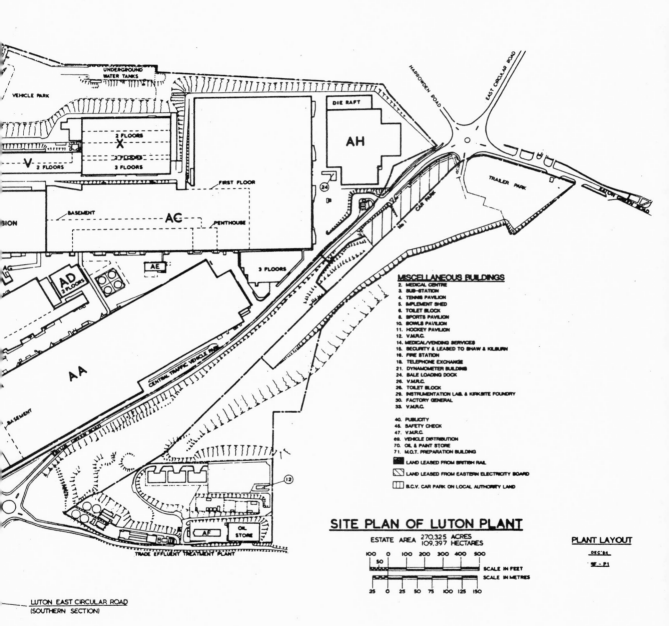

UNDERGROUND WATER TANKS

VEHICLE PARK

DIE RAFT

HARRONDEN ROAD

EAST CIRCULAR ROAD

AH

2 FLOORS
X

V
2 FLOORS

3 FLOORS

TRAILER PARK

FIRST FLOOR

CAR PARK

BASEMENT

AC

PENTHOUSE

BION

AE

3 FLOORS

AG

AD
5 FLOORS

**MISCELLANEOUS BUILDINGS**

2. MEDICAL CENTRE
3. SUB-STATION
4. TENNIS PAVILION
5. IMPLEMENT SHED
6. TOILET BLOCK
8. SPORTS PAVILION
10. BOWLS PAVILION
11. HOCKEY PAVILION
12. V.M.R.C.
14. MEDICAL/VENDING SERVICES
15. SECURITY & LEASED TO SHAW & KILBURN
16. FIRE STATION
18. TELEPHONE EXCHANGE
21. DYNAMOMETER BUILDING
24. BALE LOADING DOCK
26. V.M.R.C.
26. TOILET BLOCK
29. INSTRUMENTATION LAB. & KIRKSITE FOUNDRY
30. FACTORY GENERAL
33. V.M.R.C.

40. PUBLICITY
45. SAFETY CHECK
47. V.M.R.C.
68. VEHICLE DISTRIBUTION
70. OIL & PAINT STORE
71. M.O.T. PREPARATION BUILDING

▨ LAND LEASED FROM BRITISH RAIL

▨ LAND LEASED FROM EASTERN ELECTRICITY BOARD

▥ B.C.V. CAR PARK ON LOCAL AUTHORITY LAND

AA

BASEMENT

CENTRAL TRAFFIC VEHICLE PARK

12

AF

OIL STORE

TRADE EFFLUENT TREATMENT PLANT

# SITE PLAN OF LUTON PLANT

ESTATE AREA 270.325 ACRES / 109.397 HECTARES

**PLANT LAYOUT**

DEC'84

SE - P1

100  0   100  200  300  400  500
50
SCALE IN FEET

SCALE IN METRES

25  0  25  50  75  100  125  150

LUTON EAST CIRCULAR ROAD
(SOUTHERN SECTION)

# THE
# VAUXHALL
# STORY

# THE VAUXHALL STORY

*A Pictorial History of*
*Vauxhall Plant,*
*Cars and Commercial Vehicles*

*Richard Hart*

Farnon Books

Originally published in 1996 as
*The Vauxhall and Bedford Story*

This extended commemorative edition
published in 2002
by
Farnon Books
PO Box 248
Leighton Buzzard
Beds LU7 2JA

Typeset by GCS, Leighton Buzzard

Printed by J H Haynes and Co Ltd
Sparkford
Yeovil

ISBN 0 9511698 4 X

# The Early Days

The origins of what became Vauxhall Motors can be traced to Wandsworth Road, London, SW8, where in 1857 the firm of Alexander Wilson & Company was founded to manufacture steam engines, pumps and refrigeration plant. By 1892 a limited company had been formed. Wilson was a far better engineer than businessman and it was not therefore surprising that the company found itself in financial difficulties. Wilson resigned and set himself up as a consultant engineer. A receiver was appointed in 1896 and in 1897 the firm was renamed the Vauxhall Iron Works Company Limited.

The name Vauxhall is derived from one Fulk le Breant (also spelt Falkes or Fulkes). Through marriage, he acquired his wife's house on the south bank of the Thames. This came to be known as Fulk's Hall – corrupted over the years to Fawke's Hall, later to Foxhall and eventually to Vauxhall. The name Vauxhall survived as a district of London; the famous Vauxhall pleasure gardens were created in the 17th century near the site of the original Fulk's Hall. It was near this spot that the Vauxhall Iron Works produced its first car in 1903.

The person credited with the creation of the first Vauxhall is F. W. Hodges, who served his apprenticeship with Alexander Wilson & Company as a marine engineer. A car, which was probably a Canstatt-Daimler, was bought and studied. Two experimental belt-driven cars were made. In 1902 Hodges, in association with J. H. Chambers, who was on the board, began work on the design of the first Vauxhall car. It made its appearance in 1903 at £136. It had a 989 cc horizontal single-cylinder engine, tiller steering, single chain drive and two-speed gearbox with no reverse.

The early Vauxhall cars were very well received. One customer said of his 1904:

"The average cost has worked out at one third of the upkeep of my horse . . . an inexpensive, reliable and comfortable means of locomotion say I."

In March 1905 a *Luton News* reporter paid a visit to the newly-arrived Vauxhall Iron Works establishment in Kimpton Road. This is what that reporter wrote:

'. . . . the new works are set back some distance from the road and opening the main door, I found myself in a corridor leading to the various offices and was quickly shown into the Works Manager's room – a cosy little office, heated and lighted by electricity, and commanding a view of the whole of the extensive workshops. Mr A. E. Ash gave me a very cordial greeting and immediately put himself at my disposal.

## Established over 50 years

To get a little history of the firm was my first object and in the course of conversation I gathered that the firm which is just removing to Luton from the Wandsworth Road, London, has been established over 50 years, and until comparatively recent date was almost entirely engaged in marine engineering and pump work. From a small commencement at Vauxhall in premises which were originally a brewery, the firm has steadily increased until a change of quarters was practically forced upon them for lack of accommodation. Additional land had been built upon and all available room utilized when at last a move was decided upon, the work was being done on four storeys, the stores and engine room being in the basement and the pattern at the top of the buildings.

It was in June 1903 that the firm turned their attention to motor work, and the success attending this department quickly rendered it absolutely necessary for them to look about for larger and better equipped works. The auxiliary premises which were taken in close proximity to the Wandsworth Road Works were soon too small, in addition to which the need for concentration under one roof was recognised. Accordingly the firm cast their eyes on Luton – the advantages of which had been quite accidentally brought before them – and in due time they decided to acquire the six-and-a-half acres upon a portion of which their new works are erected. Their first production in the way of cars to bring them into prominence in the motor world was a right little car known as the Vauxhall five horse. From this they have developed to more pretentious things, and now they make nothing less than cars of the three cylinder type, and employ from 160 to 200 hands, according to pressure of work.

To a question on the difficulties of removal and an expression of surprise that they had already got so large a number at work – a glance through the window into the shop revealing a little army of workmen and plenty of machinery in full running – Mr Ash observed that they had then about 140 hands on at Luton and were gradually increasing the number week by week as the machinery was transferred from London. The process of removal had been going on in this way for some time, thus obviating any break in the output.

Chatting on business in this way, I gathered from Mr Ash that with their settlement in Luton it is the intention of the firm, in connection with the marine department to go in for motor launches, and to their motor car branch to add the delivery van business.

## Young Men at the Head

Mr Ash proceeded to conduct me through the building. Incidentally, my conductor informed me that Mr Hodges is the designer of the Vauxhall car and the head of the designing and drawing offices and I gathered that the directors of this progressive firm are mostly young men and enthusiastic in their work. Mr Ash whose special department is marine engineering, is himself well on the youthful side. He came to the firm as works manager in 1897 and joined the board two years later.

Passing into the workshop, the workmen's mess-room occupies the available space between the foreman's office and the drawing office and immediately next to the corridor. It has already been found too small, but the pressure is expected to be relieved when the workmen's cottages near at hand are occupied. A large gas cooker is provided for the use of the men.

Turning into the works at last, I found it a regular hive of industry. The building is divided into four main bays, each of 35ft span and each served with a traveller from end to end, the cranes ranging in size from one to twelve tons. Two of the bays are devoted to the marine engineering and the two on the left when entering the building from Kimpton Road are set apart from motor work.

## Electricity and Gas

The machinery are motor-driven throughout, Mr Cooke the Borough Electrical Engineer having convinced the directors of the very definite advantages of electricity over gas for power. In this connection Mr Ash spoke very highly of Mr Cooke's services. The Borough Electrical Engineer had made himself invaluable to them, nothing had been too much trouble for him to elucidate if his advice had been sought. It is gratifying to hear such testimony of a public official, and it is service of this kind which will spell success for the town's electrical undertaking. Six motors totalling 16 horse power are already in use and another of 17 horse power is being installed.

Whilst the offices are lighted and heated by electricity, the Lucas incandescent gas lamps have been utilised in the works, and the effect, Mr Ash told me, was splendid. There are also portable gas jets and tubes for each machine. The heating is by Musgrave's patent stoves.

## The Marine Department

Walking through the marine department, I learned that the firm construct engines up to a thousand horse-power and are contractors to the Board of Trade and Admiralty, the War Office, India Office, the Crown Agents for the Colonies, etc. A large amount of their trade is export to the Colonies and abroad. Just at the present moment they have not a great deal of marine work on hand, but they have over 50 motor cars, already sold, in course of making. They have just booked the machinery for two large stern-wheel steamers for the Egyptian Government.

At the railway end of the building stands the smithy with three fires from which the smoke is exhausted by fan, and there are two power hammers. Adjacent in the dispatching corner of the works, which is in the bay adjoining the railway siding are a testing plate and a testing tank.

## Motor Department

The machinery used in the motor department is naturally of a lighter type than that in the marine portion and amongst the tools we noticed boring mills, a Brown and Sharp gearcutter and Herbert's and other torret machinery for rapid reproduction of parts.

I observed that Brown and Sharp's gearcutter was an American machine, though one could not but admire its mechanism and beautiful finish. Mr Ash remarked that it was the standard gearcutter of the world and this led on to other conversation, from which I gathered that Vauxhall people are intensely patriotic and pride themselves upon every part of the Vauxhall car being British made; indeed they make every part of it themselves, except the tyres and the

bodies, and as a matter of fact, the bodies may be claimed to be made locally, as the firm work hand in hand with Messrs Morgan and Co, of London and Leighton Buzzard, in this respect. In the course of further chat, Mr Ash explained to me the various stages of manufacture of a three throw crank shaft from the rough forging to the brightly finished article.

I was next shown a large number of aluminium gear boxes and crank cases, which must have represented a considerable sum of money when one remembers that the material costs something like half-a-crown a pound. Passing by the benches set aside for the fitting up of the gear boxes and for carburettors, we next discussed the Vauxhall clutch which is a feature of the car which this firm manufactures. Its principle is to get an easy taking up of the work of the motor. There are four leather faced discs which bear on the flat of the fly wheel under spring pressure before the main cone comes into operation and the result is a perfectly easy gliding of motion for the car.

Passing next to the frame department, I was able to watch the frames being mounted with springs, axles and wheels after which they are passed on to the erectors for fitting-in of the machinery. Then, as the cars are completed, they will pass through the doorway of the main building to the running shed or garage.

## Workmen's Dwellings

The site acquired by the Vauxhall Company is, as we have said some six-and-a-half acres in extent and there is a siding from the Midland Railway running right into the works. On the frontage to the Kimpton Road have been erected eleven workmen's dwellings in addition to residences for the two foremen and a caretaker, whilst Vauxhall House, a residence of very pretty design and admirably arranged, is occupied by the Works Manager and is situated at the main entrance to the works. **)**

*A photograph of a painting owned by Messrs John Mowlem & Co. It shows the Thames river tug* John Mowlem *powered by a marine engine built by Alexander Wilson's company at Vauxhall Iron Works, Lambeth, about 1870. Marine engines were produced by the company from 1857 until 1907 when motor cars became its sole output.*

*This large power unit for a twin-paddle steamer was a typical product of Alexander Wilson. The plate on the unit says Alexander Wilson & Co, Vauxhall Iron Works, 1877.*

*The district of Vauxhall, London, at the turn of the century. The London factory moved to Luton in 1905 due to problems over the lease and lack of space. Complete cars had to be brought out of the factory basement by hoist – and the telegraphic address was Wellhole, London!*

*The original factory at Luton in 1905, which occupied a six-and-a-half acre site and employed between 160 and 200 hands according to pressure of work. The buildings on the extreme left are those of the West Hydraulic Engineering Co.*

*Vauxhall employees (above) pose for an official photograph outside their new Luton headquarters in Kimpton Road, 1905. Total workforce at this time was about 160. At the end of the First World War, Vauxhall built imposing new offices on a site immediately in front of its factory and facing Kimpton Road. The picture (below) taken in April 1951 shows the time is 5 o'clock and some of the 12,000-plus workforce are leaving for home by bus or bicycle. Today the staff that worked in the old offices in Kimpton Road have moved into Griffin House, the new head office, in Osborne Road. One feature of the old offices was a fine wood-panelled hall where a 1905 Vauxhall was always on display. Today the old offices are occupied by the Chamber of Commerce.*

*The finish of the assembly line with a Light Six on the brake adjustment machine. It was then test-driven by an expert inspector.*

*Racing motorist Kay Petrie takes a look together with officials at the new L-type 6-cylinder Velox, August 1948. Some of the workers who helped manufacture it stand in the background.*

*In 1929 the entire UK General Motors manufacturing operation was transferred to Luton from Hendon. Hendon became a centre for sales distribution and service operations. Pictured above is the Part Stores counter at Hendon. The Vauxhall Express Parts Service vans are pictured below. Both pictures were taken in the early 1930s. A few years later both departments were transferred to Luton.*

*In 1955-7 Vauxhall Motors spent £36 million to double car production. About one-and-a-half million tons of chalk and clay were excavated leaving a white plain as large as 12 football pitches, ready for the erection of a 1,600,000 sq ft building. The spoil extended Luton Airport by 12 acres, reclaimed 32 acres of marsh in Luton Hoo Park and contoured for easier ploughing 32 acres of undulating pasture in Lea Valley.*

*Block AA, early 1950s. At the time of its construction in 1948, this was one of the largest buildings in England. It was filled with modern machine tools and assembly conveyors, and produced engines, gearboxes and rear-axles for Vauxhall and Bedford cars, trucks and vans. It is said that the steelwork (1285 ft long and 480 ft wide) was imported from America where it either had been previously erected as, or was intended to be, part of a General Motors' aircraft plant during the Second World War, manufacturing the Boeing B29, the famous Flying Fortress bomber. The 5,000 tons of steelwork were loaded on a ship bound for London docks. Unfortunately a dockers' strike was in progress in London so that the steel remained on board and returned to the US East coast. It later came back to London for unloading and transportation to Luton by road.*

*The ten-thousandth Vauxhall "10" leaves the factory just five months after the introduction of the model, 1937.*

*In 1954 the name Cresta appeared on an extra-luxury version of the 2.25 litre Velox. This car is a 1956 Cresta.*

In October 1948 the first new post-war models arrived, the L-type Velox and Wyvern. These models had steering column gear change and the Velox (above) had a brand new 2.25 litre 6-cylinder engine with a top speed of 75 mph. The Wyvern had a 4-cylinder 1.5 litre engine. Both models shared a common body shell. The name of Wyvern model (below) was a surprising choice. Many people have since referred to the Vauxhall emblem as the Wyvern, whereas it is the heraldic griffin. The L-type had a rear-hinged bonnet; until that time vehicles had had their bonnets split, and hinged in the middle. Pressmen were soon to point out that "the makers have made no provision for a starting handle", as the radiator of the Velox got in the way. These L-type models were the first ever to have steering column gear change. They remained in production until 1951 when the E-type Wyvern/Velox range was introduced in 1.5 and 2.25 litre forms.

*In late 1957 the E-type Wyvern/Velox/Cresta models were replaced by long, sleek PA Sixes. The Velox and Cresta (pictured) took the 2.25 litre over-square engine. In 1959 the two-millionth Vauxhall rolled off the production line in the form of a PA Cresta. This year also saw the dropping of the traditional flutes from the body sides. They had started life on the bonnet of the 1905 Vauxhall.*

*New 6-cylinder models were on show at the 1962 London Motor Show. The PB Velox and Cresta (pictured) inherited the 2.5 litre engine of earlier PA Sixes.*

market. Almost without exception, however, styles are different from American interior furnishing.

Floor coverings – linoleum, rubber flooring, carpets and rugs – present little difficulty.

China dinner and tea services are scarce and expensive, most of the Potteries' first class output being exported. Cutlery for the home market does not yet approach pre-war standards or variety. Best quality stainless steel or silver plate is difficult to obtain. Cheap quality electro-plate is more plentiful. Household and cooking utensils, glass ovenware, etc – all can readily be obtained.

**Food**: With the exception of meat (most of which has to be imported) food supplies at present are adequate but only just! Americans will miss, however, the variety of their own diet and the essential "sweetness" of their meals; it is also likely that British cooking will be compared with some Continental and American standards and found less interesting.

Food cartons up to a specified weight limit can be imported by parcel post without duty or tax. It is recommended that canned meat, chicken and fish be included in the despatches from home. Other suggested enclosures are white flour, prepared cake flours, chocolate baking and pudding mixes; and if particular preferences are held towards canned fruits and vegetables, such items as corn, asparagus, beans, fruit salad, apple sauce, plums.

Butchers' meat, bacon, sugar, tea, butter, margarine, cooking fats, certain cheeses, are rationed in Britain. The sugar ration is almost always granulated; cube sugar, when available, must be taken as part of the ration, as must also icing or castor sugar. Flour, milk and bread are plentiful, although milk is sometimes short in the winter and temporary rationing becomes necessary. Pre-war amounts and quality of confectionery have not yet been approached – bakers' ingredients are still restricted. Cakes can be obtained without trouble, but cream and chocolate biscuits (cookies) are not easy to come by.

Unrationed coffee is in good supply. Poultry and game in season can be obtained, but turkeys usually only at Christmas time. Fresh fruit and vegetables are not so abundant as in the United States, but there are generally some varieties all the year round. Frozen fruits and vegetables are stocked by most of the larger stores. Dried fruits, particularly raisins, are comparatively scarce and most grocery stores operate their own rationing scheme to ensure fair shares. Breakfast and cooking cereals present no difficulty.

Canned foods – meat, fish, fruits, soups, etc. – are available, but not of such quality and in such variety as in the United States.

For babies, high quality powdered milks and pasteurised tuberculin tested fresh milk are available. Recommended for the food parcel, however, are bottled Junior foods for children of 15 months and over.

Shopping conditions are rather different from those in the United States. Ordinarily, in the typical suburban shopping centre there are separate shops for bread and confectionery, meat, milk, vegetables, groceries, etc. – rarely are they all under one roof. Self-service and automatic vending do not yet approach such proportions as in the United States; none-the-less, self-service in particular, is becoming popular in Britain. Milk and bread are delivered daily. (The bread will usually be unwrapped unless it is sliced). It is most usual these days for the housewife to take delivery of other food items at the shops, but regular deliveries can be obtained without much difficulty.

**Clothing**: It will be found that all clothing, as well as household linen, etc., can be purchased in graded utility quality. The small CC tab or stamp indicates that the item is free of purchase tax and that the price is controlled. Utility goods, particularly clothes, must conform to a certain specification and are often of good value, especially "top grade" utility. The word "Utility" does not do justice to some of the excellent coats, suits, dresses, etc, sold under this controlled price scheme.

**For Ladies**: Suits, with blouses or jumpers are worn all the year round, as are casual skirts with blouses, cardigans and twin sets. Woollen dresses are worn for business and home during the winter and also during cooler summer days. Cotton and silk frocks are part of any summer wardrobe, when they are worn with a light coat if necessary. The most practical and popular wear is the suit for most informal occasions, with a top coat for winter wear.

With a live hat industry, latest Paris styles are quickly copied both as expensive and inexpensive models at smaller shops and departmental stores.

Shoes are in fair supply and styles are varied. Purchase tax exemption, under the Utility scheme, also applies to shoes.

Underwear is also quite plentiful, and simple garments can be purchased at reasonable prices. There is a fair supply of nylon lingerie now on the market, but it is rather expensive as against the usual silks, rayons, etc.

Good stockings are not so easy to come by. Pure silk is expensive and scarce; nylons are also scarce and mostly not nearly so sheer as the American variety.

It is, in fact, recommended that women bring all the nylon articles they are likely to require.

Fur coats, which carry purchase tax, are of course, very costly, although there is a range of utility furs to be had.

Evening wear follows the American and Paris styles closely. In London, particularly the West End, good and stylish evening and semi-evening wear can be found to suit most purses.

**For Men**: Men in Britain dress conservatively, particularly so far as colour is concerned. Ties, for instance, are not usually so colourful or expansive. Except in really hot weather (and then only on sports and recreative occasions) the menfolk stick rather rigidly to their jackets, collars and ties, and shirts are seldom worn outside the trouser belts.

Lounge suits differ little from the American style, except that the cut is not quite so loose in an English tailored suit. All shades of grey, navy, brown and also black are usually worn, but good suiting is not plentiful and well-tailored suits are expensive.

Shirts are obtainable with separate collars (usually semi-stiff) or with collar attached, although the latter are more often only available in sports shirts. It is possible to buy shirts on the American coat style. Striped or plain white shirts are most general wear; plain white, with stiff collars being quite popular for business or fairly formal occasions. At the moment, variety and supply are not of the best and prices may appear expensive by American standards.

Although coloured and patterned socks in wool, wool mixture and cotton are available, to the American the choice will probably appear limited. For general wear with lounge suits and for business wear particularly, men seem to prefer a fairly sober patterned or even plain sock.

Locknit underwear is in good supply, although pure wool is rather expensive. It is not easy to obtain the American type of cotton under-pants, however.

The most popular headgear – soft felt "trilby" hats usually have smaller brims than those worn in the United States.

**For Children**: Clothing for children may be obtained as easily in Britain as in America – excepting, possibly, clothes for boys up to the age of five years.

Diaper-washing services are generally not available.

**Dressing**: Generally, formal evening dress (white ties for men) is now only worn on very important occasions generally. First class restaurants and night clubs in London's West End often require evening clothes, but dinner jackets are more usually worn than tails. On the whole the war years have left behind a casual attitude towards dressing in the evening and the necessity for evening clothes will be rare.

Before you have been long in Britain you will want to know how much things cost. How much you will have to pay for commodities and how much butter, cheese, bacon and meat your rations will allow you. You will want to know how our cost of living compares with the American. This four-page supplement has been prepared to answer those questions and to give you some idea of current prices. It should be remembered that rationing fluctuates slightly and that all prices are rising. However, as a generalisation you will find that setting up a home costs about as much as in the States, but that living expenses are not so great. *'*

---

### Household ration per year in S.E. England

| | | *from* | | | *from* |
|---|---|---|---|---|---|
| Coal | 34 cwt | 5s 7d cwt (cwt = 112 lbs) | Coke | as available | 5s 5d cwt |

### Other Items (unrationed)

| | | | | |
|---|---|---|---|---|
| Bread 6d (large loaf – just under 2 lbs) | | | Motor spirit | 3s 8d gallon (1 Imperial gallon – 1.2 American) |
| Milk | | 6d pint | | |
| Coffee | | *from* 5s 0d lb | Pipe tobacco | from 4s 0d oz |
| Cigarettes | | *from* 3s 8d for 20 | | |

### Equivalents

| | |
|---|---|
| £1 (one pound) = 2.80 dollars | 1d (one penny) = 1 cent (approx) |
| 1s (one shilling) = 14 cents | |

### Accommodation

| | *from* | | *from* |
|---|---|---|---|
| Houses to buy with vacant possession | £2,500 | Houses to rent (furnished) | £9 a week |
| Board residence, private houses | £5 a week | Apartments to rent (furnished) | £7 a week |
| Board residence, hotels | £8 a week | | |

### Domestic Help

| | | | |
|---|---|---|---|
| General help, living in | *from* £3 a week, plus board | Daily help | 3s per hour |

### Furniture and Household Goods

| | | | |
|---|---|---|---|
| Dining room suite | £75 | Gas washing machine | £40 |
| Lounge suite | £80 | Electric washing machine | £100 |
| Bedroom suite | £85 | Radio (table model) | £30 |
| Carpet (square or centre) | £30 | (licence required – £1 a from any Post Office) | |
| Carpet (fitted) | £80 | | |
| Cooker | £30 | Radiogram (licence as above) | £70 |
| Electric refrigerator | £120 | Television | £75 |
| Gas refrigerator | £70 | (licence required, £2 a year for radio and television) | |
| | | Hire of radio | *from* 5s a week |
| | | Hire of television | *from* 15s a week |

### THESE GOODS ARE RATIONED

| | | | | |
|---|---|---|---|---|
| | Beef | | 2s 6d lb | |
| | Lamb | (Individual ration to | 2s 6d lb | (Average price |
| Meat | Pork | value of 1s 7d per week) | 2s 6d lb | according to cut) |
| | Veal | | 2s 0d lb | |

### Individual ration per week

| | | | | | |
|---|---|---|---|---|---|
| Butter | 3 ozs | 2s 6d a lb | Bacon | 3 ozs | *from* 2s 11d a lb |
| Sugar | 10 ozs | 6d a lb | Margarine | 4 ozs | 1s 2d a lb |
| Candy | 6 ozs | *from* 3s 0d a lb | Lard (cooking fat) | 4 ozs | 1s 4d a lb |
| Cheese | 2 ozs | *from* 2s 0d a lb | Tea | 2 ozs | *from* 3s 8d a lb |

*Staff of lacquering shop, 1916. Mrs Nellie Burley is in the middle of the first row. Also in the picture is foreman Bill Smith, who later took over a garage in Stuart Street. Mrs Burley was 16 when the photograph was taken. She worked at Vauxhall as a material handler during the whole of the First World War and then was employed in a number of local hat factories. During part of the Second World War she again worked as a material handler.*

*The sombre faces of the workers in the above picture contrast strongly with the smiling Vauxhall employees seen below who are saying that they are "fit for work".*

*The year is 1935 and the only women employees, except a few employed on inspection work, are to be found operating these rapid-moving powerful sewing or trim machines.*

*Employees of Plant maintenance and Project blocks Y and Z, about 1945. Back Row: Reg White (fifth from left). Front Row: Mr Girdlestone, Charles Archer, Alf Sargent, Mac Smith and Ernie Nicholls. Others include Jimmy Launders, Jim Smith, "Jimmy" King, Tom Unstead and R H Bygrave.*

*The comptometer section of the Luton cost office, April 25 1961. Pictured, left to right, are (front row) Dorothy Linsdell and Mary Phillips; (second row) Hazel Battams, Yvonne Buckingham, Pat Whitworth; (third row) Gillian Davis, Joan Collins, Pearl Kilmister; (fourth row) Beryl Smith, Mary Stobbs, Jean Richardson; (fifth row) Eileen Telford, Doris Chlad, Joyce Parker; (sixth row) Christine Walker, and standing on either side of the supervisor Marion Hawkins are Rosemary Thompson and (next to window) Marion Buddon. Marion Hawkins was the supervisor for many years.*

*George Brown, Bill Staples, Fred Howlett and Ron Meers with a Vernons Pools cheque for £87,879.75. They were part of a seven-strong syndicate in Material and Production Control who each won over £12,000 in 1990.*

*Employees celebrate the Cavalier back as the number one best seller in the UK, February 1990. Pictured are Sharon Leon, Brian Groom, Jim Davis, Gordon Mead, Chris Grzesczuk, Pam Hopkins, Shirley Batchelor, Wally Lupton, Max Cooper and Geoff Willmott.*

*In December 1990 commemorative presentations were made by Paul Tosch to the following 25-year employees, most of whom are pictured above: R. Bastable, C. Common, J. D. Barrett, R. M. Brewer, A. R. Currington, J. Hurst, E. Manton, J. M. Nutkins, J. P. Roberts, P. D. F. Sterne, V. F. Shepherd, M. C. Pressland, T. M. Pearce, T. E. Carlisle, R. C. Dale, T. P. Dobbyn, R. S. Pepper, K. Patel, B. J. Brown, C. J. Gordon, T. J. Jones.*

*Every item of specification added to Vauxhall cars at Luton and Ellesmere Port results from a plan produced in Griffin House. Specification includes colour and trim of vehicles, car badges, seat belts, and even the glove box light. Decisions are based on market research and cost. The team suggests to Opel and GM's European designers what should be included in the British models. Pictured are the Product Planners in 1991: Ernie Hooper, John Winter, Wendy Grey, Phil Harwood, John Rutherford, Martin Lay, Paul Confrey, Stuart Harris.*

*Dave Hall (centre) and colleagues Roy Adams and John Beal with their fire vehicles and the Vauxhall ambulance. They are part of the Luton Fire and Security Department. The fire unit deals with some 1,300 calls a year, from both within and outside the plant. During the summer they have an average of two grass fires a day on the nearby railway tracks which jeopardize Vauxhall property on the south side of Kimpton Road.*

*Tom Reilly won £130 under the Employee Recognition Scheme for his idea to reduce the size of paint pots he uses. Only a tiny amount of paint was needed each week. Previously this paint was held in large pots which cost more than a pound each, and in which the paint went hard quickly and had to be thrown away. Tom is pictured in July 1991 with the old, large bottles and the new tiny ones.*

*Luton Mayor Cllr Ray Sills opens Vauxhall's Heritage Centre in May 1993. With him are company director Tony Burnip, Tony Spalding and Vauxhall's oldest living former employee, Lewy Norris, 98. Lutonian Lewy Norris started work at the car plant in 1915, just ten years after the factory opened. A former commercial department employee, he signed the company's first £1 million cheque to the government during his 44 years with the firm.*

*Paul Tosch, former Chairman and Managing Director.*

*Charles Golden, who was Chairman and Managing Director from 1993 to 1996.*

# Social and Sporting Activities

Charles Bartlett, who was Managing Director from 1930, followed a policy of promoting men to positions of responsibility from off the shop floor. Bartlett saw social and sporting activities as an important way of demonstrating the skills necessary for management. He helped promote drama and sporting facilities. Peter Vigor recalls in an interview with Len Holden: "If you wanted to get on with Bartlett you had to take an interest in the Recreation Club. For example you might take up tennis and sit on the Tennis Club Committee and become chairman. This showed Bartlett that you could organise." The Vauxhall Recreation Club used to have some 30 sections which included everything from minor hobbies to sport and horticulture. Many activities took place in the huge canteen which fronted Kimpton Road. Peter Vigor recalled his own personal record for the *Luton News* Vauxhall Souvenir Supplement:

‘The canteen was not a beautiful building, although the steps at the front and the facade were impressive. It was constructed like a huge aeroplane hangar. At the time it was built it was considered a colossus, but it was soon too small for the company's requirements and a further large two-storey extension was stuck on the end of it.

Whereas the original roof was 40 feet or so high, with plenty of skylights, the addition was only 15 feet high, with no roof windows, its ceiling being the floor of the weekly-paid staff canteen, which was transformed into a ballroom or what was called the Vauxhall Theatre when the occasions arose.

Under the extension it was often dark, dungeon-like. It probably spoiled the architect's sense of proportion. It certainly did not add to the beauty of the interior.

There were other canteens in this complex: the hourly-paid and weekly-paid (which included monthly), the directors' dining room and the management group dining room.

The kitchens, serveries and offices were extensive as there were three meal-breaks a day for the day shift and three for the night shift. I estimate well over 10,000 meals a day were served when the factory was working full out, not counting snacks at breakfast and tea times.

The bar room included six billiards tables, dart boards and an indoor skittles alley, and committee rooms and a shop.

There was a fully-equipped stage with dressing rooms, and showers that could be used at any time. Badminton and table tennis sections of the Rec Club were regular users, but they were available to anyone who worked in the company.

When it was demolished it was not so much the heaps of bricks and mortar which saddened me, but the thoughts and memories that went through my head.

During the war I used the main canteen for my meals and snacks. The food was of high quality and the kitchens spotless. Food rationing never bothered me because five or six days a week I had my main meal in the canteen.

I also enjoyed monthly dances, table tennis, badminton and boxing shows there. At Christmas and on sports days the canteen was decorated and used for the celebrations. Those occasions were quite a sight, something like the Tower Ballroom at Blackpool!

The staff canteen ballroom floor was sprung maple, and Sir Reginald Pearson, president of the rec club and of the social section, was very proud of this floor, and had it protected with a heavy canvas drugget. He threatened dire consequences if he found anyone dropped a cigarette end on this covering or on the floor. To think that a demolition firm swung a concrete dolly over this floor and dropped it time and time again until the maple was mere firewood to be burned on site . . . sacrilege!

Another feature of this great clumsy building was the four or five murals behind the serveries in the hourly-paid canteen.

These were painted during the war by a woman artist commissioned by the rec club through David Jones, the styling manager. I understand someone took a picture before they too were demolished. The murals depicted the fishing industry, harvesting and other scenes reminiscent of the food chain. I loved those paintings, not because I thought them masterpieces but because there among the clamour of cups and cutlery rattling on enamel-topped tables, and queues of boiler-suited workers, they reminded me of fresh air and the peaceful countryside.

I doubt if many Vauxhallite memories are of art, or peace and quiet in the main canteen. And yet . . . what about the symphony concerts, when the London Philharmonic Orchestra under Sir Adrian Boult and other mainline conductors filled the canteen to capacity? Hard chairs cost a shilling (5p) and there were a few armchairs at 2s 6d (12.5p). Nobody grumbled about the seating.

But the noise of the crickets, the draughts and the distance from the town centre of Luton finally made the Vauxhall music section move to the more comfortable seating arrangements at local cinemas, like the Alma, Odeon and Savoy.

There was home-produced music too, for Fred W. Green organised Sunday concerts with stars from the London variety theatres. The male voice choir and the girls choir joined the Vauxhall Concert Orchestra, and then the big stage had to be extended by an apron to accommodate the whole cast.

Theatrical shows in the staff canteen drew large audiences. The average was three shows a year, farce, comedy or drama, including a production of Shakespeare's Taming of the Shrew.

Each Christmas there were two or three children's parties, with employees volun-teering for all kinds of duties, from clowning to marshalling the hundreds of noisy and rumbustious youngsters. I remember when Sir Reginald Pearson took off his coat to load the children on to a log slide. In later years children demanded more sophisticated entertainment, and were taken to pantomimes, at Oxford and London.

One of my earliest memories of the canteen was the flower, fruit and vegetables piled almost to the ceiling for shows of the horticultural section and supported by Messrs Andrews, landscape gardeners of Leagrave.

And the art exhibitions – 500 pictures by employees from all departments, and once including five by managing director Sir William Swallow. Photographic exhibitions, badminton and table tennis tournaments, brass band competitions . . . sometimes these events were so popular they almost took over the canteen for a weekend.

There was even a dog show, which was banned after only one year because Arthur Adams, the canteen manager, objected to it on hygienic grounds.

Sometimes the company used the main canteen for long-service gold watch presentations, management group meetings, presentations for safety, savings and accident-free driving. There were huge dinners for the 25-year club.

In the general council room all the larger club committees met, under photographs of Sir Charles Bartlett and Sir Reginald Pearson. They had been keen supporters of the recreation club, and both were Presidents.

The pensioners used this room for business meetings, and the staff canteen for monthly social evenings.

Sometimes the canteen was too popular. Sparrows loved the warmth and the crumbs. The management tried many means to get rid of them – owls, bird lime and traps among them.

But like me they were enthusiasts. They got far more out of Vauxhall Motors than just scratching a living. ❜

*The Dunstable Annual Christmas party, 1964. William Swallow, M. A. Aldridge, A. F. King, C. F. Davidson, A. Bourn, N. Maskell and their wives were amongst the merrymakers. Music was provided by the Ramblers Orchestra and the MC was Keith Mayles.*

*Pensioners' Annual Christmas party at Luton on December 4 1990. Six hundred pensioners and their wives attended the annual event making it a complete sell-out.*

*Enjoying a laugh: Barbara Row, Kathleen Essex, Works Manager David Cato, Sylvia Curtis, Neil Gardner, Shirley Batchelor and Alec Curtis, Christmas 1990.*

*Ted Read thanks Tony Lines, Personnel Manager, for the management team's hard work at the Pensioners' Christmas party, 1990. From left: Joy Young, Janet Lines, retired director David Young, Tony Lines, Ted and Olive Read.*

## Sporting Activities

*Athletic Club swimming section 1916-17 (above) and Athletic Club football team, 1918-19 (below).*

At the Motor Show, Olympia, 1905, pictured above, 434 types of car were displayed at an average price of £600 with the most expensive costing £2,500. The Vauxhall stand can be seen in the foreground. Pictured below is the 1993 Motor Show at Earl's Court with the Vauxhall stand in the centre. At the 1905 show in November, Vauxhall introduced its first 4-cylinder car, an 18 hp motor costing £475, whilst at the 1993 Motor Show it displayed the Tigra concept car powered by a 1.6 litre ECOTEC engine and the Traka. The idea was to evaluate public response to these two new potential models and then decide whether to manufacture one or both vehicles.

*The evolution of the Vauxhall logo. The heraldic 1920s griffin was based on the crest of Fulk le Breant who was granted the manor of Luton by King John. Through marriage le Breant owned property in Lambeth on the south bank of the Thames where the Vauxhall Iron Works was later built. His Lambeth house and grounds were called Fulk's Hall, corrupted over the years to Fawke's Hall, later to Foxhall and ultimately Vauxhall. When in 1857 the Scottish engineer Alexander Wilson set up a business at the Vauxhall Iron Works in south London, he took the griffin as his company badge. The griffin badge returned to Luton when the company moved out of London in 1905!*

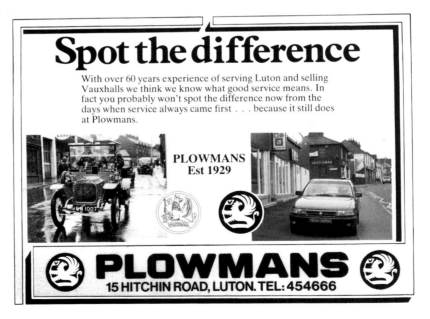

*Plowmans, Hitchin Road, Luton, advert, 1991. The petrol pumps had to be removed in the 1980s owing to fire regulations and the canopy was removed to make way for cars.*

On Saturday afternoon, June 6 1953, Lutonians thronged the streets from Manor Road to Wardown to watch the Coronation procession wind its way along. Nearly 70,000 people saw the Vauxhall Motors' carnival entry.

A Vauxhall car being taken ashore in a surf boat, Accra, Ghana. Before the war the Hendon factory was used as Vauxhall's Export Boxing plant – the place where cars and trucks were packed for shipment overseas.

*This silver salver has inscribed on it all the victories won by the Vauxhall team between 1909 and 1925. It is interesting to note that the salver was made by melting down most of the trophies awarded to the firm's drivers during those years.*

*A 1904 Vauxhall completes the hill climb run by the Sporting Owner Drivers' Club in Woburn Park, 1968.*

*Manx Trophy Rally, 1977. Finnish team leader Pentti Airikkala wins for Dealer Team Vauxhall in a Blydenstein-tuned 2300HS Chevette. Risto Virtanen is in the passenger seat.*

*Tina Thorner and Louise Aitken-Walker celebrate victory in the 1990 RAC Rally. Louise Aitken-Walker was the first woman home, finishing 17th overall and clinching the FIA Ladies World Cup. She won the two-litre class by a massive 35 minutes in her Astra 16v.*

*Formula Vauxhall Lotus action at Donington Park, 1990. For the 1991 season Vauxhall Motors and Mobil provided a prize fund and support package worth over £12,000 for the 15-race championship of the Vauxhall 2-litre, 16-valve cars.*

*The late Dave Metcalfe takes the Nova to 14th spot in the tough 1,400 mile four-day event RAC Rally in 1990.*

*Vauxhall's formula junior car. This took to the tracks for the first time in 1991 with a support package and prize fund of over £40,000. The 1600 cc Nova GSi-engined single seaters were a favourite choice for those seeking a first step on the motor racing ladder of success.*

*1993 Corsa Rally Cross car pictured at the Motor Show. For the technically minded it has a Corsa 3-door bodyshell, 1600 cc single cam engine developing 160 bhp at 7,000 rpm. The car is fitted with a corbeam seat, 5-speed gearbox and Avon rallycross control tyres with a strengthened roll cage. It has MacPherson struts with de Carbon dampers, uses Mobil 1 oil and Mobil unleaded fuel and weighs 700 kg.*

*Vauxhall display at the 1993 Motor Show with Vauxhall sport karting (foreground) for 8-12 year olds. Speeds of 50 mph can be obtained. In the background is the Dallara 393 Formula 3 racing car with a Vauxhall 2-litre, 16 valve twin overhead cam.*

*Tom Behan, boiler operator, checks the dials of boiler No. 1 at Ellesmere Port, 1967.*

*Another milestone in 1981 was the start of Astra production at Ellesmere Port, earlier Astras having been imported from Opel. The Cheshire plant was now building both Chevette and Astra ranges.*

*Prime Minister John Major presents on behalf of management a silver salver to Works Manager, Mike Chapman, marking Ellesmere Port's record output in 1990, which he received on behalf of all the work-force. Picture taken February 1991.*

*In February 1990 the new buzz-word at Ellesmere Port plant was continuous improvement. The engine trim area was the first to give the revolutionary new work process a try.*

*New press shop, Ellesmere Port, about 1991. Using state-of-the-art technology, and weighing 1,600 tonnes, this Large Transfer Press carries out the work of four conventional press lines and produces up to 16 body panels per minute. It takes just 33 hours after the first piece of steel is pressed for the finished car to leave the line, fully inspected and tested.*

*New paint shop, Ellesmere Port, about 1991. Verification operators closely examine the paintwork on the Astra to ensure that the high quality controls and degree of mirrored finish from the advanced paint formulations are maintained at all times.*

*1935: Assembling Bedford engines at the Luton factory where Vauxhall cars and Bedford trucks were designed and made.*

*One of the first Bedford two-tonners at work in 1931. This one is the shorter version – 131 in wheelbase (WHG). For five months this particular truck carried pipes for a Rhondda Valley sewage scheme along the bed of the River Taff.*

*1936 Bedford 12-15 cwt van, 22 hp owned by J. Ovel from Soursham, Huntingdon, pictured at Woburn Abbey in 1991.*

*The original flat-nosed Bedford undergoing Army trials shortly before the start of the Second World War. The vehicle allowed certain non-standard truck items to be housed under the bonnet.*

*1941 Bedford 4 x 4 QL military GS C owned by R. Woodcock, Ampthill, pictured at Woburn Abbey in 1991.*

*Rt Hon G. R. Strauss, MP, Minister of Supply, drives the 500,000th Bedford off the assembly line at Luton, Wednesday, October 22 1947. In his speech to the workers he emphasized that every car exported meant a week's meat ration for 10,000 fellow citizens. Also in the cab of the Bedford was the Vauxhall employee, Arthur Fountain, who had driven off the very first Bedford truck ever built, back in April 1931.*

*In April 2001 twenty Plant employees were treated to a retirement lunch hosted by Diana Tremblay, Director of Manufacturing. Unit managers were also in attendance. The retirees were: John Dennis, David Thompson, Brian Naylor, Roy Porter, Dave Edwards, Ivor Johnston, Barry Skerman, Ray Kirk, Geoff Martin, Peter Smith, Roy Vincent, Peter Horsler, Bob McAllister, David Carter, Les Dilley, Peter Keymer, Robert Tompkins, Malcolm Pakes, David Thompson and Jim Stewart.*

*The 1999 Chairman's Honours Certificates were awarded at a gala dinner in the Riverside Suite at the Vauxhall Recreation Club. The Luton Plant team for that year were awarded for their contribution to providing Life Long Learning Opportunities within the Plant.*

*May Ball, 2001 celebrating 75ᵗʰ anniversary of the Vauxhall Rugby Club. Rugby and football have been played in Luton since 1905 when works teams, usually farmers or people working in the then thriving hat trade, played informal games with no real rules. (Top row): Joe Webber, Kevin Green, Mark Bushby, Paul McIntyre, Gary Sherry, Craig 'Rumble' Day, Pat Fitzpatrick, Andy Raynor, Gary France, Steve Maclaughlan Snr., Andy 'SOS' Savage, Steve 'Beau' Dayer, Jason Kell. (Bottom row): Steve Maclaughlan Jnr., Jamie Gardiner, Leo O'Neill, Darren Maclaughlan, and Dave Munn.*

*Vauxhall Athletic Club, runners and coach Des Haughney (front, right) with some of their trophies, 1998. The club trains regularly at The Brache and has around 130 runners aged from ten to 70.*

*Paint Unit at Luton Plant reached 85 per cent quality "first time OK" on a shift, 2001. Pictured at their quality meeting are Roger Parton (supervisor), Alan Davies, Mark Fenn (supervisor), Robin Dolby, Dave Boyce, Paul Sibley (shift manager), Ian Woolfe, Abdul Parker, Paul Gobey, Steve Dorbon (supervisor), Ian Barrett and Dave Worker.*

*A robot-training cell for Body Unit was designed and built by this five-man project group from Maintenance. Pictured in 1998 are (back row): Mick Hodgkinson, Alan Godfrey and Paul Harris. (Front row): Danny Stone and Ali McGuinness.*

*In April 1997, this lucky syndicate of twelve Body Unit Maintenance men won £4.9 million or £413,585 each, in the National Lottery. The* Vauxhall Mirror *reported that they all planned to stick around Vauxhall. Syndicate leader Dave Roberts said: "Of course it will change our lives – there shouldn't be any overdraft worries, or moaning about the bills. I suppose I'll do the usual sort of things – buy a villa in Spain or something – but I'm still finding it hard to take in. I just sit on the sofa and look at the numbers."*

*Luton Body Unit dash line team headed by Dave Swan and Sean Lake, produced no fewer than 45 ideas, all of which were implemented. Cash rewards were paid, up to 20% of the first year's savings. Pictured in 1997 are team members John Protaszczak, Percival Townsend, David Swan, Ranford Powell and Ralph Ogden.*

*Apprentices and junior operators receive their certificates from Works Manager David Cato after successfully completing their formal training. The apprentices' BTec college course enabled them to become fully qualified maintenance engineers. The six junior operators are now fully qualified production operators. Also pictured are Barry Robson their training officer at Vauxhall (front left) and Mike Sanderson (front right) of the Engineering Training Authority.*

*Pop superstar Paul Young (second right) with former Luton Plant colleagues, Cliff Huson, Paul Gassor and Bill Baldry, 1996. Paul, who hails from Luton, spent four years with Vauxhall in the early 1970s serving a craft apprenticeship as a toolmaker in the old Die Unit (X-Block). He left in 1976 to develop his music career.*

*Luton Plant in conjunction with the Recreation Club, played host in 2001 to sixteen children from the Chenobyl Children Lifeline, Luton and Dunstable link. All the children were from the Ukraine and the event involved fun and games at the club.*

*Guidelines award ceremony at The Brache, May 1999 with Baroness Blackstone, Director of Luton University and Nick Reilly, Vauxhall Chairman. This event was also to celebrate the partnership of Luton University and Vauxhall Luton Plant's Guidelines Centre.*

*As part of the European Health and Safety Week in October 2000, a children's poster competition was held. The three winners and their families came into the Plant to receive their prizes and meet a very special guest!*

*Luton Plant Family Days were great fun but involved a lot of organising. They were usually held every two years. Pictured above in the light coloured suit is Director of Manufacturing, John Barber. Some ten years later the paint shop operatives are dressed as the ugly sisters.*

Jonathan Moore
Karen Morris
Yvonne Parkar
Garry Stubbs
Steven Thomson
Herold Wallace
Thomas Buckingham
Debra Edwards
Tracey Hagger
Ram Jassi
Raymond Lanceley
Neil Martin
Paul Martin
Geoffrey Parsons
Stephen Ricketts
Stella Ridgwell
Purshatam Rupall
Steven Simms
Paul Solomon
Pravin Vara
David Wall
Peter White
Bimla Bhatia
Victor Dobson
David Foster
Michael May
Brian Rumbold
Paul Thomson

1989

Stewart Ashby
Lee Bagnall
Mohammed Bashrat
Charanjit Bhullar
Stephen Brown
Daksha Chauhan
Tanya James
Carol Palmer
Philip Potts
Muzamel Shah
Harish Solanki
Andrew Walton
Alison West
Philip Arrowsmith
Danny Bayne
Simon Healy
Lydia Larkin
Pravin Mistry
Harjinder Theara
Gloria Anderson
Ujibai Cuchhadia
Stephen Harrison
Joseph Kerr
Abdul Khalifa
Mohamed Khalifa
Gary Marchant
Michael McCormack
Steven Moore
Paul Philip
Amanda Rawson
Susan Seaborn
Tina Wallace
Paul Wigfield
Stephen Harfash
Lorna Lynch
Jay Mathias
Christine Turner
Stephen Collier
Peter Dalton
Michael Dobinson

Jasbir Lidder
Paul Lomax
Sajad Mahmood
Shanta Odedra
Pushpa Robinson
Narinder Sidhu
Derek Atkinson
David Boyle
Philip England
Mark Hodges
Alison Thomas
Stephen Wilkinson
Paul Baldwin
Denise Barbi
Kevin Barker
Hatim Bharmal
Frederick Bullard
Clive Bushen
Simon Collar
Shaun Eldred
Alan Eldridge
Steven Garrett
Raymond Gear
Rocco Graziano
Colin Maskell
Shirley Aquart
Gerald Franks
Zhara Nour
Murad Parkar
Audrey Simmons
John Sleet
Robert Watts
Sheikh Abdin
Paul Allen
Finlay MacKenzie
Steven Minter
Anil Patel
Kishor Rajput
Barrington Stamp
Kobir Uddin
Pauline Cleary
Peter Coyle
Peter Douglas
Raymond Flitton
Lee Kingsland
Mahmoud Kokabi
Anthony Newton
Leslie Brum
Derek Flemons
David Gransby
Douglas Hardy
Paul Naylor
Robin Phair
Mark Pollard
Sandra Potter
Ragini Sharma
Baffour Awuah
Dean Bellinger
Richard Day
Alan Edge
Roy Foster
Brian Fox
Keith Harding
Michael Johnson
David Longhurst
Stephen Munns
Steven O'Brien
Alexander Robinson
Wlodzimierz Rozylo
Paul Smith
Paul Stevens

Timothy Sutch
Martin Akhurst
Martin Billings
Shaun Gallagher
Paul Malahoo
Michael McConkey
James McLean
Loretto Smith
Keith Young
Michael Atkins
Emanuele Campaniello
Michael Costello
Loyell Donaldson
Jonathan Hendy
Jhulman Lidder
Malcolm Plaats
Gabriel Rebeyro
Keith Smith
Linda Allen
David Dawes
Annette Henry
John Kerr
Gary Love
David Medwynter
David Moules
Nicholas Reville
Bogumila Rozylo
David Box
Graham Bygrave
Lynda Cummins
Michelle Farrell
Delwyn Gorvett
Gulam Hussain
Robert Jones
Steven Jones
George Laird
Lien Lam
Gordon McCreadie
Julie Moss
Eva Moynihan
Tracey Roberts
Darren Scowen
David Shepherd
Ronald Stanger
Gary Stapleton
Kevin Brooksby
Kevin Fleckney
Harbham Keshwala
David Laverick
Balwant Maju
Eugene Martinez
James Mullin
Joseph Murtagh
William Nagle
Andrew Baron
Graham Crouch
Domenico Ferraro
Andrew Golding
Andrew Hill
Rosemary Hussey
Abu Jamal
John Morris
Graham Newson
Owen Savage
Archie Vaughan
Mark Vincent
Kenneth White
Steve Adrien
Inder Assi
Catherine Daws
Robert Hill

Bader Khan
Tariq Mahmood
Mahesh Mistry
Manmohan Singh
George Smith
Shirish Vyas
Howard Wedderburn
Robert Chrystie
Harvinder Dhami
Kulvinder Gill
Barbara Mantell
Shaun Palmer
Alan Ridley
Shoaib Sarwar
Andrew Saxby
Dale Yarwood
Kanta Zala
Vinh Lam
Mumtaz Ahmed
Palvinder Buttar
Paul Freeman
John Gibbs
Ian Harley
Valerie Hartgill
Terence Hennessey
Michael Hurst
Kanubha Jadeja
David Kirby
Andrew Pearson
Jagir Rai
Narinderjit Singh
Douglas Soames
Subhashchandra Talati
Kenneth Wright
Gary Archer
Keith Bennett
Russel Clarke
David Downham
Stephen Drury
Robert Fensome
Christopher Finn
Paul Fitzgerald
Eric Giles
Sharaz Hussain
Jamshaid Khan
Amrik Mann
Ahmed Mohamed
Mark Sullivan
Patrick Tyrrell
Amanda Wells
Balbir Basra
Gary Deamer
Dave Ferguson
Edward Fountaine
Philip Hughes
Martin Hyde
Hue Lam
Vinh Lam
Timothy Loader
John Lock
James McGovern
Michael Newman
Daniel O'Donnell
Michael Sully
Kenneth Ward
Trevor Chance
Kevin Foster
Richard Gray
Teresa Jakins
Vinh Lam
Alan McCabe

Francis Pugh
Alan Rea
Ravi Robinson
Calvert Seaton
Paul Vincent
Beverley Williams
Simon Bozier
Anthony Few
Andrew Flanagan
Derrick Hart
Phi Hoang
Simon Lodder
Choudhary Mahmood
Sadiq Quazi
John Reeve
Chhinder Sandhu
Monica Carrera
Jarnail Chattha
Isaac Fevrier
Keith Golding
Denis Herrity
Zulqar Nain
Andrew Rankin
Michael Williams
Frank Bedford
Eric Bradshaw
John Brown
Timothy Houghton
Peter Pearson
Kevin Scales
Mehmet Suyolcu
James Bhowmik
Richard Broughton
Peter Bygrave
Terence Cain
David Carraher
Abdul Chikte
Kelly Doxsey
Darren Evans
Carlo Gelmini
Satnam Jandu
Harbans Kaur
Nigel Lacey
Adrian McCorkell
Paul Mitchell
Bharat Patel
Brenda Revitt
George Rosemorgan
Laslo Seress
Anne Townrow
Alan Upton
Darryll Birkin
Christopher Bride
Pradrip Gareja
Robert Hills
Arthur Jarvis
Joan Johnson
Adrian Knight
Angela McAndrew
Sundar Miah
Govindbhai Mistry
James Mitchell
Shamim Munir
Nora Naughton
Darren Palmer
Stephen Scott
Usha Sekhon
Natwarsinh Solanki
Leonard Wilson
David Turner
Nathan Appleby

Roderick Arnold
Ian Bennett
Deborah Bryce
Robert Byrne
Thomas Carroll
Perbinder Gill
Satinder Gill
Rakesh Gohel
Nicky Hammond
Jameel Masih
Christopher Morris
Jaswinder Sandhu
Geoffrey Sarney
Paul Snook
Dave Strain
Ian Warboys
Terence Ward
John Wood
Lennox Browne
Tracy Burdekin
Jason Cuthbert
Andrew Dockerill
Neil Gay
Paramjit Gill
Stephen Jenkins
Shebul Miah
Mervyn Rogers
Clive Sinclair
Charles Turner
Dawn Turpin
Ian Warner
Anthony Wright
Mohammed Zafar
Steven Deamer
Kevin Fake
Satnam Kandola
Nadeem Khan
Hansaben Mistry
Patrick Proudfoot
Laurence Richmond
Mark Rowe
Derek Scott
Basha Singh
John Solecki
AnthonyVaughn
Richard West
Donna Buckingham
David Burnss
Permjit Chahal
Babu Chavda
Andrew Gainsford
Lap Lang
Chang Luu
Van Luu
Van Luu
Donald Parrott
Raymond Roberts
Denis Rutter
Anthony Simpson
Mohammed Uddin
Cleveland Campbell
Robert Evans
Paul Fitzgerald
Richard Harris
Derek Horne
David Martindale
Roger Pannell
Anthony Scantlebury
Christopher Stock
Darren Stratton
Mohammed Ahad

Anthony Earthrowl
Shahid Iqbal
David Jenkin
Nigel Kemp
Meherban Khan
Simon La-Fortune
Kevin Lennox
Robert Letham
Robert Mahon
Praful Parmar
Ibrahim Yeboah
Nicholas Bailey
Kevin Hennelly
John Jackson
Shamriz Khan
David Kiddy
Giovanni Lombardi
Anthony Slinn
Patrick Tufft
Trevor Watson
Rohel Miah
Abdul Pazeer
Parwinder Soora
Nahim Yasin
Darshan Chahal
Kamaljit Dhillon
Mark Fountain
Chun Li
Stephen Maguire
Antony Makepeace
Chor Mo
Gary Nolan
Mansoor Rathor
Darren Welsh
David Williamson
Alex Blair
Paul Brown
Manjit Chahal
Harpal Chana
Ravinder Chana
Darren Davies
Tyrone Hoyte
Nicholas Hunt
Andrew Lowes
David Northeast
Gordon Riley
Keeley Winch
Nickolas Zissis
Brian Anley
Anthony Armstrong
Mark Brennan
Anthony Butcher
Paul Butler
Steven Crichton
Steven Dumpleton
Stephen Golding
David Johnson
Vinh Luu
Mai Ly
Alan McDonagh
Sever Musumeci
John Scoon
Tracey Whitehead
Derek Ashwell
Abdul Basith
Veronica Golding
Jonathon Hake
Jean Hughes
Mohammed Ilyas
Edward Kirkpatrick
Christopher Kordek

Ian Morris
Andrew Moss
Kevin Owens
Bhadresh Patel
Stuart Pinkney
Huutai Tran
Michael Dear
Simon Huckstep
Mohan Kainth
Alan Kightley
Aroop Nandre
Martin Ward
Enrico Fabbro
Susan Wheddon
Richard Fuller
Aziz Khan
Justin Oliver
Michael Rawson
Paul Rummery
Blackford
Patrick Nelson
Nhat Thi
Mohammed Motlib

1990

Joseph O'Sullivan
John Quirke
Brian Walker
Stephen Peirce
Lee Bacchus
Alan Batchelor
Anthony Farrell
Ivor Fitzpatrick
Juan Jimeno-recio
Shahbaz Khan
Daniel McHugh
Edward Shanley
Susan Andrews
Paul Brown
George Green
Graham Leggatt
Andrew West
Ian Boddy
Patrick Galvin
Michael Holmes
Carol Jefferson
Mark Nelson
Nagajan Odedra
Vincent Perry
Ronald Robertson
Richard Watson
Simeon Ogunji
Dennis Davies
Basakha Dheer
Brian Goodchild
Ginder Manak
Alexis Morby
Jeremiah Murphy
Norbert Page
Gary Power
Ian Russell
Lynda Sewell
Aslam Shah
Martin Smith
Adrian Beswick
Malcolm Blake
Mohanlal Ramsumair
Michael Read
Joseph Robertson
Amanda Victor

Yash Balley
Carole Boston
Mark Brookes
Gurdial Chahal
Alan Martin
William O'Neill
Karl Sadlier
Mark Savage
Andrew Smith
William Waldock
Jasbinder Bains
Peter Butler
Daniel Carroll
Patrick Carroll
Danny Conway
David Douglas
Jacinta Fahy
Luninging Ferris
Gul Hayat
Wellesley Lewis
Linda Lifford
Edward Locke
Mohammed Merban
Richard Moulding
Peter O'Mara
Ibrar Hussain Shah
Steven Shead
Eraldo Tuveri
Barry Denton
Stuart Elmer
Mohammed Amin
Ronald Burnham
Eriel Callender
James Cast
Nicholas Cavallo
Russell Clark
Dhiraj Darjee
Ciaran Das
Jose Hernanz
Darren Hucklesby
Ramesh Kumar
Mark McLaughlin
Sharfuddin Mullaji
Tracey Reid
Jason Reilly
Leroy Roberts
Beatrice Rosser
Kevin Rouse
Mark Rust
Gurdip Singh
Harjit Singh
Mark Turner
John Allard
Neil Atkinson
Richard England
Candy Frith
Surjeet Kalsi
James Manson
Dennis Martin
Russell Martin
Martyn Oliver
Anthony Crummey
Alan Fursman
Vincent Kelly
Michael O'Malley
Dale Pillar
Colin Seager
Brian Watts
Ian Batchelor
Martin Benson
Graham Cook

Dominic Henry
Anthony Munden
Harvey Nichols
Gary Smith
Philip Wood
Michael Day
Maxwell Levy
Simon Bellinger
James Bradley
Jayed Choudhury
Yvonne Fitzgerald
Karl Hagger
Nicholas Jones
Ajaz Khan
Dennis Maguire
Nigel McVey
Richard Mead
Joseph Monahan
James Morgan
Lee Murray
Michael O'Brien
William O'Donnell
Scott Reading
Jacqueline Whittick
Nigel Bird
Graham Blake
James Cronin
Ziaul Islam
Surinder Johal
Dalvinder Marwaha
Bhavesh Patel
Andrew Warren
James Watts
Colin West
Justin Archer
Stuart Benson
Margaret Cloonan
Neil Fitzjohn
Derek Hale
Mary Rooney
Michael Semo
Dale Skerman
Zyghunt Sterecki
Charlie So Tran
Anthony Watkins
Nicholas Whitehead
Nichola Wigfield
Terry Wrettom
Vera Clarke
Andrew Crook
Mohammed Haque
Abdul Kalam
Adrian Leyden
Majella McLaughlin
Sahajahan Miah
John Napper
Julie Pye
Wayne Schonewal
Robert Thrussell
Gillian Turner
Sean Wallace
Felix Akuoko
David Beagle
Kevin Bell
Jason Black
Robert Bruce
Japhtha Butler
Martin Egan
Robert Field
Alan Jones
Jan Jude

Christopher Lawson
Shahan Miah
Kevin Millard
Vito O'Shea
Gordon Renton
David Rozentals
Graham Turner
Shawn Ayles
Ian Burrett
Andrew Dunbar
Satnam Flora
Colin Jackson
Mizanur Khan
Andray Lewis
Jason Nimmo
Ali Raza
Mark Summers
Stephen Williams
Robert Windows
Robert Beeson
Surinder Chahal
Liam Cooke
Resham Dhillon
Stephen Farr
Shabbir Karachiwa
Stephen Knox
John McGrath
Shirley Moss
Philip Newman
Paul Rowe
Darshan Sehgal
Stephen Sherwood
Kuljit Singh
Karter Singh
David Smith
David Williams
Carmel Yang
Anthony Brown
Mark Carroll
Brenda Holloway
Jeremy Holt
Clinton Howell
Paul Keely
Alice Law
Paul McIntyre
Barbara Warren
Manzoor Bhatti
Brian Briston
Robert Claridge
Margaret Fyall
Stephen Gower
Tahir Khan
Muhammed Munshi
Michael Osborn
Robert Provan
Keith Seager
Rodney Smith
David Stanbridge
Carl Beaney
Terry Dayman
Luciana Giugno
Darren Grace
Mark Hargreaves
Narendra Mistry
James Ongley
Alan Sage
Paul West
Thomas Birks
Baljit Chohan
John Collins
Albert Dumpleton

Robert Farquharson
Howard Geary
Sally Hamill
Gurpal Kaur
Daniel Nixon
Rajinder Pawar
Glyn Smith
Andrea Tortorella
Michael Turner
Graham Watson
Anwar Ali
Gianluigi Cossu
Wayne Day
Stephen Johnson
Jamie Law
David Williams
Martin Pennewitz
John Glazebrook
Gary Hargreaves
Christopher Hart
Mohammad Latif
Andrew Meade
Bradley Poore
William Stewart
Roberta Wooton
Robert Wright

**1991**

Martin Cummins
Maurice Kiss
Geoffrey Mason
John McGrattan
Andrea Ruberto
Marion Fitzgerald
Philip Hill
Vincent Pietropinto
Kenneth Hulm
David Fulcher
Tony Day
Frank Hemmings
Simon Protheroe
Daniel Stone
Robert Turner
Imran Bashir
Claire Belmar
Iain Dewar
Rakesh Gandhi
Paul Harris
Kevin Meatyard
Robert Sherlock
Paul Treanor
Christopher Gillies
James Howells
Campbell McManus
Julian Coles
Anthony Holmes
Mark Saunders

**1992**

Lee Bryan
Edward Clark
Stephen Gamble
Joseph Greene
Ikram Hussain
Nicola Lunnon
Craig Powell
Graham Protheroe
Terence Simmons
Christopher Stirrup

Paul Weston
Matthew Godfrey
Paul Kelly
Scott McLachlan
Andrew Mudie
Eamonn Sheridan
Denis Bailey
Paul Brill
Damon Clarke
Richard Connolly
Sukhvinder Dhalliwal
Anthony Negus
Kevin Pillar
Danny Stockley
Ian Willmott

**1993**

Ana Azevedo
Neil Armstrong
James Botham
James Collins
Simon Dear
Kendrick Edwards
Jon Gibson
David Harding
Terence Hardy
Zoe Horton
Alison Jones
Darren Lanouette
Jason Mardle
Michael McAree
Taimur Miah
Alan Morris
Terence Philpott
Aaron Reynolds
Ricky Scott
Neil Treanor
Angela Williams

**1994**

Ian Walker
Garry Clarke
Anna Clews
Roger Davidson
Neil Delaney
Sarah Farrell
Aminul Haque
Steven Harris
Steven Holmes
Adam Hughes
Luke Jarvis
Mark Logue
Robert Slater
Mark Martin
Nigel Mckeown
Kletos Pantazi
James Payne
Kelly Powell
Neil Simmonds
Kevin Standbridge
Jonathon Whiting
Neil Woodman
Roger Thompson
Richard Harris

**1995**

Brian Birmingham
Holger Gericke

Jonathan Gregson
Alastair Cassels
Jeremy Roberts
James Wilson
Martyn Beazley
Lee Caswell
Michael Coggins
Jon Dains
Michael Dawson
Gary Duffy
Russell Gibbins
Keith Grant
Jonathon Horne
Matthew Isaac
Sam Leitch
Neville Matthews
Darren May
Liam Murphy
Richard O'Meara
Danny Parrott
Terry Rolt
Stuart Sullivan
James Taylor
Benjamin Walker
Benjamin West
John Bailey

**1996**

Steven Baldwin
Keith Batt
David Creed
John Dalton
Barry Davies
Paul Kelly
Lyndsay Knight
Simon Moore
Noel Morgan
Mushtaque Parkar
Adrian Parrott
Hasmuk Vara
Paul Clarke
Brent Donoghue
Steven Green
Andrew Hettle
Colin Hoare
Peter Markey
Gary Mead
Gary Rogers
Raymond Stewart
Susan Suttle
Matthew Webb
Christopher Yates
Jason Boniface
Mukesh Dhiman
Adrian Foote
John Gamble
Sam Ha
Mark Peek
Andrew Robins
Steven Tearle
Dean Adams
Thomas Bennett
Anthony Burridge
John Crimmins
Darren Curl
Julie Gill
Keiron Griffin
Michael McIntyre
Khalid Miah
Andrew Morris

Brian Nelson
Jayant Patel
Tarun Patel
Miles Redman
Dean Saunders
Graham Stimpson
Ian Woulfe
Keith Brailsford
Ian Camp
Ronald Clarke
Bryan Coyle
Steven Crawley
Martin Davies
David Dickinson
Alan Dobbs
Russell Doherty
Mark Harrison
Brian Huggett
Israr Hussain
Christopher Ivey
Kam Jagpal
Colin Kirk
Jason Land
Robert Leach
John McEvoy
Paul Merricks
Naresh Nahar
Colin O'Byrne
Robert Owens
Leigh Parkins
James Sadlier
Ian Salter
Robert Sedgewick
Peter Smith
Dale Stokes
David Tebbitt
Paul Wright
William Bangs
Matthew Brandon
Liam Carroll
Joseph Croft
Tara English
Trevor Glenister
Mark Hammond
Susan Holdham
Pauline McGee
Philip Nash
Sandra Smith
Anita Smith
Leslie Ward
Robert Watts
Graham Wells
Badrul Ahmed
Mohammed Ashraf
Narinder Bains
Graham Baldwin
Prabjot Bhungal
Stephen Bradbury
James Chadburn
Stuart Colbert
Jason Cooper
Lloyd Goodall
Caroline Green
Ben Griffiths
Keith Groom
Daren Hall
Declan Hennessy
Syed Khan
Andy Kimber
Pauline Miles
Andrew Milne

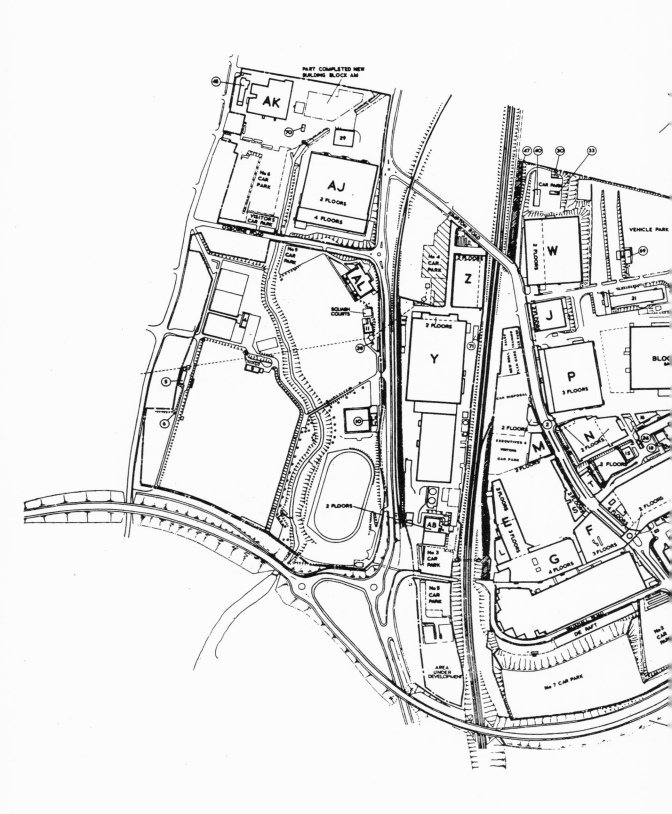